Seasons and the Sun

Lisa J. Amstutz

Rourke Educational Media
A Division of Carson Dellosa Education

BEFORE AND DURING READING ACTIVITIES

Before Reading: *Building Background Knowledge and Vocabulary*

Building background knowledge can help children process new information and build upon what they already know. Before reading a book, it is important to tap into what children already know about the topic. This will help them develop their vocabulary and increase their reading comprehension.

Questions and Activities to Build Background Knowledge:

1. Look at the front cover of the book and read the title. What do you think this book will be about?
2. What do you already know about this topic?
3. Take a book walk and skim the pages. Look at the table of contents, photographs, captions, and bold words. Did these text features give you any information or predictions about what you will read in this book?

Vocabulary: *Vocabulary Is Key to Reading Comprehension*

Use the following directions to prompt a conversation about each word.

- Read the vocabulary words.
- What comes to mind when you see each word?
- What do you think each word means?

Vocabulary Words:
- *equator*
- *orbit*
- *sun*
- *tilts*

During Reading: *Reading for Meaning and Understanding*

To achieve deep comprehension of a book, children are encouraged to use close reading strategies. During reading, it is important to have children stop and make connections. These connections result in deeper analysis and understanding of a book.

 Close Reading a Text

During reading, have children stop and talk about the following:

- Any confusing parts
- Any unknown words
- Text to text, text to self, text to world connections
- The main idea in each chapter or heading

Encourage children to use context clues to determine the meaning of any unknown words. These strategies will help children learn to analyze the text more thoroughly as they read.

When you are finished reading this book, turn to the last page for an **After Reading Activity**.

Table of Contents

What Are Seasons?

Seasons change each year.

Weather can change with the seasons.

In spring, the air warms up.

Seeds sprout.

The summer **sun** is hot.
The days are long.

Plants grow fast.

In fall, leaves turn colors. They drop to the ground. The days grow short.

Snow falls in winter. The weather is very cold. But soon, spring will come!

Around the Sun

Earth circles the sun.

Each **orbit** takes one year.

Why do the seasons change? It is because Earth **tilts** to one side.

Different parts of Earth are closer to the sun as Earth circles.

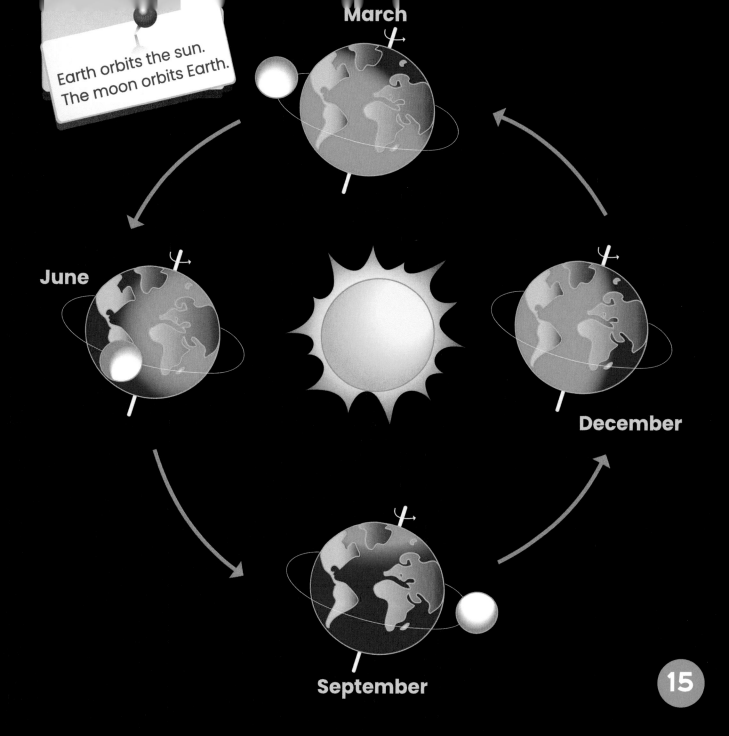

Earth orbits the sun.
The moon orbits Earth.

March

June

September

December

15

North and South

The **equator** is an invisible line. It splits Earth in half.

One half is in the north. The other half is in the south.

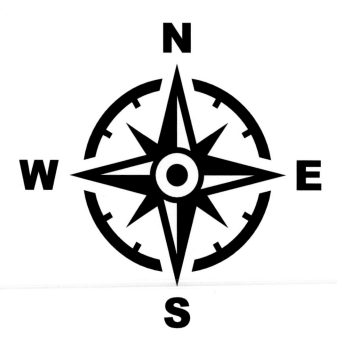

Equator

At the same time of the year, the north and south have different seasons.

When the northern part of Earth tilts away from the sun, the southern part of Earth tilts toward the sun.

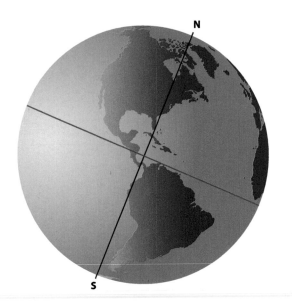

Winter in the north happens at the same time as summer in the south.

Winter starts in December in Arizona, United States, in the north.

Summer starts in December for Sydney, Australia, in the south.

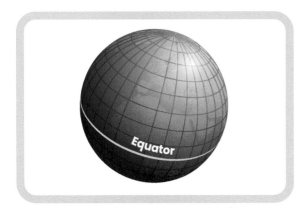

equator (i-KWAY-tur): An imaginary line around the middle of the Earth.

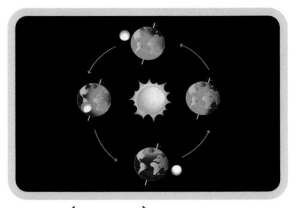

orbit (OR-bit): The curved path followed by a moon, planet, or satellite as it circles a planet or the sun.

sun (sun): A star the Earth orbits around.

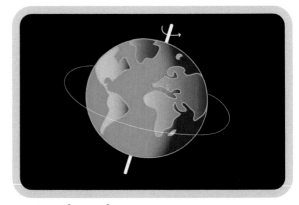

tilts (tilts): Leans or tips to one side.

Model the Seasons

Make a model of Earth. Use it to learn how the seasons change.

Supplies

permanent marker   orange   toothpicks (2)   flashlight

Directions

1. Use the marker to draw a line around the middle of the orange. This will be the equator.

2. Stick a toothpick in the top and bottom of the orange. These will be the North and South Poles.

3. Hold the orange straight up and down. Turn off the lights and shine your flashlight at the orange. Observe: Where does most of the light fall?

4. Now, tilt the top of the orange toward the light. Observe: Where does most of the light fall now? Does any light hit the poles?

5. Try tilting the bottom of the orange toward the light. What changes do you see?

Index

About the Author

Lisa J. Amstutz is the author of more than 100 children's books. She loves learning about science and sharing fun facts with kids. Lisa lives on a small farm with her family, two goats, a flock of chickens, and a dog named Daisy.

After Reading Activity

What season is it where you live? Write down the time the sun rises and sets. How many hours of daylight did you record? Track the times for a week. Are the days getting longer or shorter?

Library of Congress PCN Data

Seasons and the Sun / Lisa J. Amstutz
(My Earth and Space Science Library)
ISBN (hard cover)(alk. paper) 978-1-73163-847-2
ISBN (soft cover) 978-1-73163-924-0
ISBN (e-Book) 978-1-73164-001-7
ISBN (e-Pub) 978-1-73164-078-9
Library of Congress Control Number: 2020930188

Rourke Educational Media
Printed in the United States of America
02-2412211937

Edited by: Hailey Scragg
Cover design by: Rhea Magaro-Wallace
Interior design by: Jen Bowers
Photo Credits: Cover logo: frog © Eric Phol, test tube © Sergey Lazarev, p4 © Moncherie, p5 © BlueLine, p6 © Rawpixel Ltd., p7 © Martinns, p8 © Dee Browing, p9 © skynesher, p10 © FERRAN TRAITE, p11 © alexkich, p12 © titoOnz, p14 © puflic_senior, p15 & 22 © milena moiola, p16 & 22 © lukaves, p17 © leonello, p18 sun © Vitalii Bondarenko, Earth © PeterHermesFurian, p19 © mkarco, p20 winter background © Ikan_Leonid, Grand Canyon © Spondylolithesis, p21 summer background © Lemon_tm, Sydney, Australia © PhotoAllel, All interior images from istockphoto.com.